THE BIG TREE

WITHDRAWN

THE BIG TREE

written and illustrated by
BRUCE HISCOCK

Atheneum   New York

COLLIER MACMILLAN CANADA
TORONTO
MAXWELL MACMILLAN INTERNATIONAL PUBLISHING GROUP
NEW YORK   OXFORD   SINGAPORE   SYDNEY

Atheneum
Macmillan Publishing Company
866 Third Avenue, New York, NY 10022

Collier Macmillan Canada, Inc.
1200 Eglinton Avenue East
Suite 200
Don Mills, Ontario M3C 3N1

Printed in China
10 9 8 7 6 5 4 3

Library of Congress Cataloging-in-Publication Data
Hiscock, Bruce.
The big tree / written and illustrated by Bruce Hiscock.
— 1st ed.   p.   cm.
Summary: Follows the development of a large old maple tree from
its growth from a seed during the American Revolution to its
maturity in the late twentieth century.
ISBN 0-689-31598-8
1. Trees—Juvenile literature.   2. Trees—Life cycle—Juvenile
literature.   [1. Trees—Life cycle.]   I. Title.
QK475.8.H57   1991   582.16—dc20
89-18286   CIP   AC

1775   1800   1825   1850   1875

To Everett and Jim, keepers of the big tree

1900   1925   1950   1975   2000

*A*utumn had come again to the big tree. As the days grew shorter, the dark green leaves changed to yellow and gold. For a while they clung to the branches, and the tree was dazzling and bright.

Then one frosty morning, the leaves began to fall. Down, down they drifted onto the tin roof of the old farmhouse. Winter was on the way, and the leaves were no longer needed. Soon the big tree would shed them all.

The big tree is a sugar maple. It stands high on a hill in northern New York State, by the last farmhouse on a dirt road. Sugar maples are common trees there, but few ever grow to this size.

The massive trunk of the old maple is over four feet thick, and its branches rise a hundred feet in the air. It is a giant tree now and still growing. But of course, it wasn't always so big.

Long ago, around the time of the American Revolution, this tree began as a small seed.

Most of the country was wilderness then, and an ancient forest covered the spot where the farmhouse now stands. Wolves prowled silently in those woods. Eagles glided overhead, and tall evergreens swayed in the wind, brushing their needles against the broad leaves of the hardwood trees.

Some of those hardwoods were maples, and one fall they released thousands of winged seeds.

The seeds whirled and spun as they fell. Some landed on the rocks and some in the brook. One seed, no different from the others, came down on a patch of good soil and was covered by falling leaves.

The seed did not sprout, though, for sugar maple seeds must be chilled by the winter before they are ready to grow. Soon the cold days came, and a blanket of snow pressed the seed to the ground.

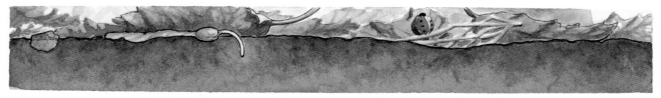

In the spring, when the sun warmed the earth, a slender white root pushed out of the seed.

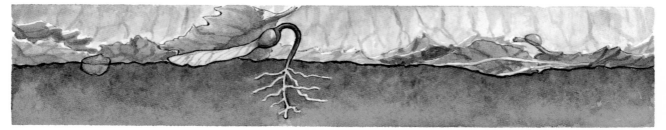

As the root grew into the damp soil, the tiny stem began lifting the seed from the ground.

The seed split open, and a long pair of seed leaves unfolded.

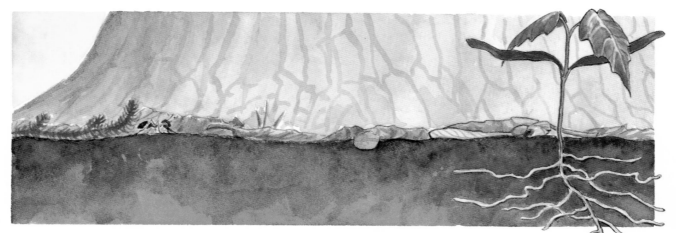

In a few days the true maple leaves appeared, and the big tree was on its way. The year was 1775.

That same spring Paul Revere made his famous ride, and the American colonists began fighting the British. It was the start of the Revolutionary War.

The next summer, as the fighting continued, the Americans declared their independence from England on July 4, 1776. The tree was just a year old. Later a fierce battle was fought in the valley below the hill, but the war never reached the old forest.

The maple grew very slowly during this time, for huge trees sheltered the seedling, keeping the forest floor dark and shady. After six years, the tree was only as tall as a rabbit.

Then one spring, when George Washington was president, a violent storm swept over the hill. It knocked down an old white pine, and for the first time, bright sunshine reached the little maple. The tree began to straighten and lift its leaves toward the light.

The maple grew steadily after that. In a few summers it was much taller than the seedlings in the shade. Like all green plants, the tree was using energy from the sun to make its own food.

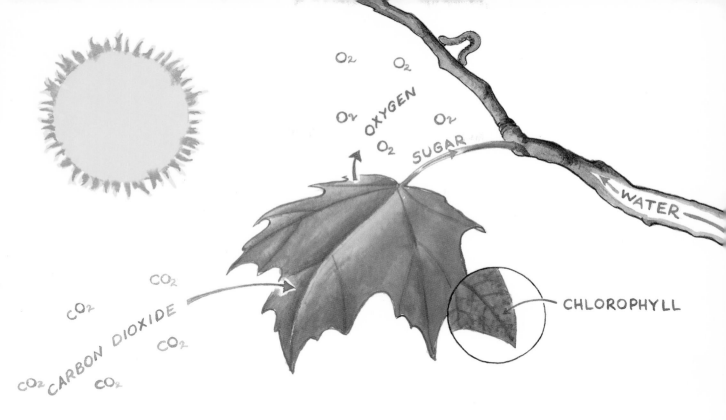

Trees make sugar, their basic food, by a process called photosynthesis. The sugar is produced in the leaves, which gather sunlight. During photosynthesis the leaves combine water, supplied by the roots, with carbon dioxide gas from the air. Sugar is formed, and oxygen, the gas that we and all other animals breathe, is given off. This wonderfully complex process is carried out by chlorophyll, the substance that makes leaves green.

Some of the sugar produced is used right away as food for the growing tree, and some is stored. The rest is transformed by the chemistry of the tree into cellulose, the tough fiber in wood, leaves, roots, and bark. And so the tree makes all of itself, even its strongest branches, starting with air, rainwater, and a few minerals.

In the early 1800s, when the tree was about thirty years old and the United States was spreading westward, loggers came to the ancient forest. With sharp axes, they cleared most of the hillside to make a farm.

When they reached the place where the tree stood, the owner of the land said, "This is a good site for a house. Save that fine maple for my yard."

So the tree and a few others were not cut.

Once in a while a logger would pause in his work to count the rings in the stump of a tree. Trees grow bigger around by adding a new ring of wood each year. By counting them the logger could tell the age of the tree. Some of the stumps had over three hundred rings.

In the spring, as the little leaves emerged, carpenters began building the farmhouse. The work went slowly, for everything was done by hand.

They finished the outside, nailing plain cedar shingles on the back and fancy pine clapboards on the front, just when the trees were turning. As the green faded from the leaves of the big tree, the brilliant colors that were hidden all summer came shining through.

When the house was done, the leaves lay on the ground like an old brown carpet. Eventually they would rot, returning their minerals and adding compost to the thin mountain soil.

Forty years passed. The nation expanded to twenty-eight states while the big tree grew taller and thicker and added new limbs. Underground it grew a strong set of roots as well. The roots near the trunk held the tree firm against the wind, while smaller roots spread as wide as the branches to collect water and minerals from the soil.

Trees need enormous amounts of water. Inside a tree, water carries minerals up to the leaves and sugar back down to the roots and other parts of the plant. These watery mixtures are sap, the lifeblood of trees.

Sap travels through a network of tiny tubes somewhat like our own blood system. But the tree has no pumping heart to move the sap around. Instead, water in the sap evaporates from each leaf and twig. As this moisture is lost, more water is drawn up from the roots to replace it. On a sunny day gallons of sap water are lifted up to the leaves as the sap circulates throughout the tree.

For many years the farmer collected sap from his maple trees to make syrup and maple sugar. By 1865 the big tree had become an excellent producer, but the farmer had grown old. Now his grandchildren, back from the Civil War, did the sugaring.

In March, when the first thaw came, they tapped the trees by drilling holes in each trunk. The holes were not deep, for the sap flows in the sapwood just under the bark. A spout, called a spile, was hammered firmly into each hole and a bucket attached. On a warm day the sap ran with a steady *drip, drip* while the chickadees sang their spring song.

When the buckets were full, the sap was poured into an iron kettle and boiled down. It takes about forty gallons of the slightly sweet sap to make a gallon of syrup.

Sometimes a bit of syrup was boiled longer and then poured onto the snow to make a sweet, chewy candy.

The sugar that sweetened the sap had been stored all winter as starch in the roots and trunk of the tree. Now that spring was near, the sap flowed through every branch to awaken the tightly closed buds.

After a few weeks the buds began to swell. That's when the sap turns bitter and the sugaring season is over.

By early May the tree was filled with small maple flowers.

The flowers produced pollen, and the pollen floated on the breeze to other maple blossoms. Later many of those flowers would develop into maple seeds.

The leaves opened next, stretching out with the tender young branches, making the tree a little taller.

The tree grew on into the twentieth century. There were forty-eight states in the Union now, and automobiles began chugging up the hill. The farmhouse was over a hundred years old, and its age was showing.

The maple was old, too, but solid and healthy. It had neither been struck by lightning nor lost a big branch to the wind, and so the bark had never been badly injured. Bugs often chewed on the leaves, but the covering of bark protected the wood from insects and rot.

Then, in the fall of 1987, an early snowstorm hit the hill. Heavy, wet flakes clung to the leaves, bending the branches until they could stand no more.

Snap...thump! A large limb crashed down on the yard. Then, *whump,* another fell, and another after that. The snow continued all day. The sound of breaking trees was like rifle fire in the woods.

It will take many years for the maple to recover from that storm. For a time some of the inner wood—the heartwood, which is no longer alive—will be exposed to the air. But gradually, new bark is covering the scars. The tree was damaged, but it survived.

As the tree has aged, life on the hill has changed, too. No one farms the rocky land anymore. Most of the cleared fields have grown back into forest. Even the road was moved, so now the tree stands in the backyard. But the house has been fixed up again. It has electricity, indoor plumbing, and a VCR.

Now, every Fourth of July, neighbors and friends gather under the big tree for a picnic to celebrate the birthday of America. Over two hundred years have passed since the Revolution, and this maple has weathered them all.

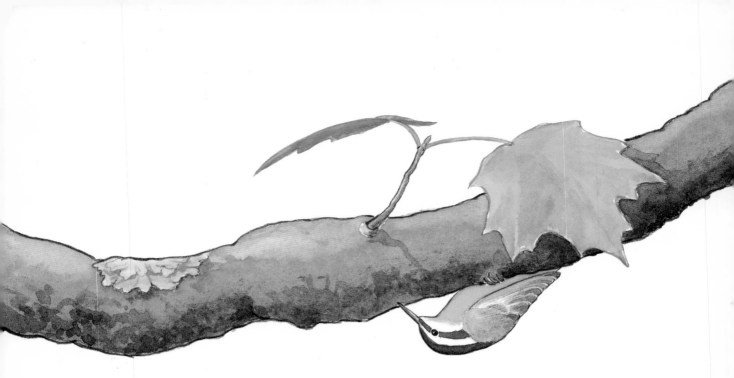

The big tree is very old now, but still strong and growing. With a bit of luck, and clean air and water, it will go on shading picnics for many more years.